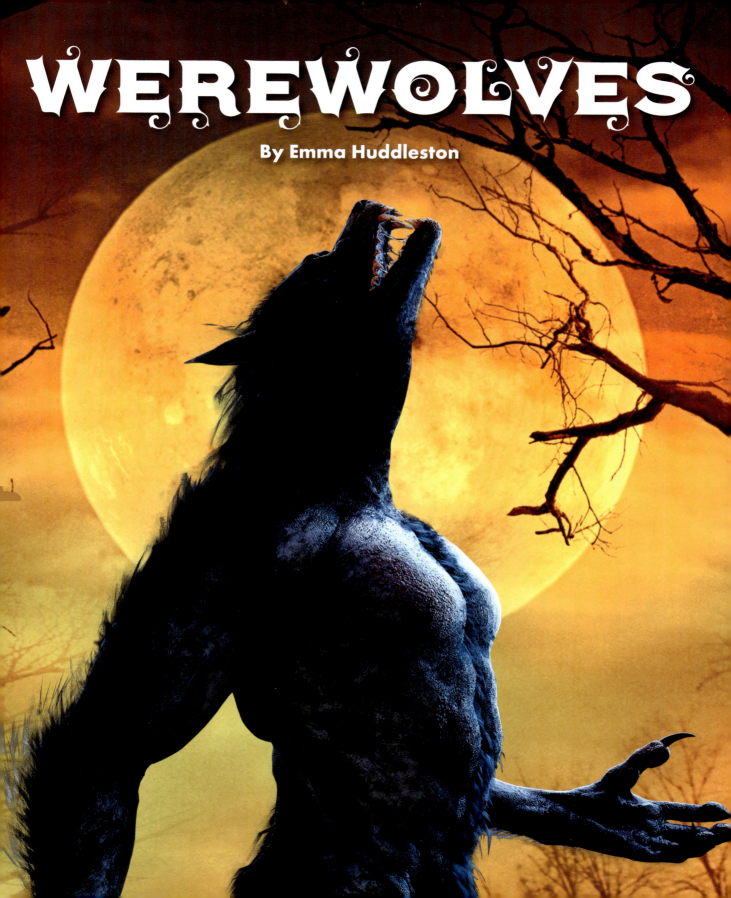

Published by The Child's World®
1980 Lookout Drive • Mankato, MN 56003-1705
800-599-READ • www.childsworld.com

Photographs ©: iStockphoto, cover (werewolf), 1 (werewolf), 9, 17, 19; Shutterstock Images, cover (background), 1–3, 12, 15, 23; Virrage Images/Shutterstock Images, 5; Richard Seeley/Shutterstock Images, 6; Edwin Tan/iStockphoto, 7; Ershova Veronika/iStockphoto, 10; Daniele Gay/Shutterstock Images, 13, 24; Denis Simonov/Shutterstock Images, 16; Universal Pictures/Album/Newscom, 20; Kathy Hutchins/Shutterstock Images, 21

Copyright © 2022 by The Child's World®
All rights reserved. No part of this book may be reproduced or utilized in any form or by any means without written permission from the publisher.

ISBN 9781503849822 (Reinforced Library Binding)
ISBN 9781503850859 (Portable Document Format)
ISBN 9781503851610 (Online Multi-user eBook)
LCCN 2021939637

Printed in the United States of America

Table of CONTENTS

CHAPTER ONE

Howling at the Moon...4

CHAPTER TWO

History of Werewolves...8

CHAPTER THREE

Hairy Beast...14

CHAPTER FOUR

Werewolves Today...18

Glossary...22

To Learn More...23

Index...24

CHAPTER ONE
HOWLING AT THE MOON

The full moon shone down on the green tent. A brother and sister unzipped the door and climbed inside. They laid out their sleeping bags. They heard their mother put a log on the campfire. The wood crackled and burned. They crawled back out of the tent to roast marshmallows.

While they were roasting marshmallows, they could hear crickets chirping. The tall trees in Yellowstone National Park looked like shadows. Suddenly, they heard a wolf howling in the distance. The kids looked at each other with wide eyes.

People must be careful while camping. They might run into wolves.

Wolves are an important part of Yellowstone's environment. They are protected inside Yellowstone National Park.

    The howling reminded the girl of a scary story. She began to tell it. She told her brother that werewolves are said to be legendary half-human, half-wolf creatures. They have long black fur and bright yellow eyes. She said that werewolves fed on human children. Her brother said that he heard werewolves had been sighted in the United States! Their mother shook her head. She told them werewolves were not real. But everyone flinched when they heard the wolf's distant howl again.

People have been telling stories about werewolves for thousands of years.

CHAPTER TWO
HISTORY OF WEREWOLVES

The core part of all werewolf legends is that people turn into wolflike creatures. Some fully become animals. Others are part human, part wolf. They can still think or talk like a human. The main difference from story to story is how someone transforms from human to werewolf. Most modern werewolf stories show werewolves changing form during the full moon. But legends throughout history are different.

Stories about werewolves are different around the world. But they all involve wolflike creatures.

In some werewolf stories, people put on wolf pelts to transform into wolves.

Early werewolf legends come from Greek and Norse **mythology**. The poet Ovid wrote *Metamorphoses* around 8 AD. His poem included many Greek myths, including the legend of Lycaon. King Lycaon tried to trick the god Zeus by feeding him human **flesh**. But Zeus was not fooled. He punished Lycaon by turning him into a wolf forever.

In an old Nordic legend, men put on pelts to become wolves. Pelts are animal skins. The story emphasized the difference between humans and animals. In these stories, the men care about each other when they are human. But when they are animals, they could attack anyone.

In a legend from Germany, a man puts on and takes off a belt to turn from man to wolf. He has control of the change. He is not **cursed** or punished like people in other legends. Additionally, he can go back and forth between creature and human.

A legend from South America says the seventh son in a family of all boys will turn into a werewolf. The change happens during a full moon. This legend is well-known in Argentina, Brazil, Paraguay, and Uruguay.

The full moon is an important part of many werewolf stories.

CHAPTER THREE

HAIRY BEAST

Werewolves are known as hairy creatures. They have powerful and strong bodies like real wolves. They are known for their speed and animal senses. Their sharp sense of smell helps them hunt.

Werewolves look similar in legends around the world. Their large, hairy appearance is based on that of wolves. Wolves have a tail and sharp teeth. They walk on four legs. In some werewolf stories, werewolves look like regular wolves. But legends from South America were different. They told of werewolves that looked more like hairy, **deformed** people than wolves. Eventually these stories mixed with European legends. The creature became half human, half wolf.

The appearance of werewolves is largely based on that of wolves. For that reason, their appearance doesn't vary greatly from country to country.

Different stories show the human side of werewolves in different ways. Spoken tales described the creatures as having the ability to think or talk like a person. Later on, movies showed creatures that shared some physical features with people. Werewolves in movies often walk on two legs.

Stories say that werewolves are vicious.

Werewolf legends describe the creatures as bloodthirsty. This means they want to kill people. Sometimes they kill other animals, too. Bloodthirsty behavior was linked to being evil. People believed only evil creatures would attack and eat human flesh.

Many stories also show werewolves howling at the moon. It is possible this came from real wolves. Wolves howl to communicate with each other. The loud sound travels far distances. A wolf can share its location or warn others if a threat is near. The howl can also show where **prey** is located. However, wolves do not howl at the moon.

Wolves may howl at any time, not just when a full moon is in the sky.

CHAPTER FOUR
WEREWOLVES TODAY

Sometimes animals **inspire** legends. Wolves were hated in Europe, where many werewolf legends started. Wolves were large, dangerous **predators**. People feared wolves in real life and werewolves in legends.

People have inspired werewolf stories, too. Some of these people were criminals. Others were later identified as having a mental illness. Peter Stubbe was a German man from the 1500s. He claimed to be a werewolf. But he may have actually had lycanthropy (ly-KAN-thruh-pee). This is a rare mental disorder. People who have it believe they are an animal, sometimes even a werewolf.

Other illnesses besides lycanthropy have inspired werewolf legends. Hypertrichosis (hy-pur-trih-KOH-sis) is a rare disorder that causes extreme hair growth. Someone with this condition might look like a werewolf to other people. Rabies is a disease that causes brain swelling, fever, madness, seizures, and death. Someone with this condition may act like an animal or unlike themselves. Hallucinations are imaginary people or places that someone believes to be real. They can be caused by mental disorders or drugs. People experiencing hallucinations may be convinced they have seen a werewolf.

Fear of wolves inspired many werewolf stories.

Eventually, legends from around the world mixed. Werewolves became popular in stories, books, movies, and music. One of the first werewolf movies was *The Wolf Man*. It was made in 1941.

Lon Chaney Jr. played the Wolf Man in the famous 1941 movie. He also played the role in the many sequels that followed.

David Thewlis played Remus Lupin in the Harry Potter *movies. This character is a werewolf.*

From 1997 to 2011, the *Harry Potter* books and movies came out. They had a werewolf character. He changed every time there was a full moon. He couldn't control his behavior when he was a wolf. So he kept himself away from people when he transformed. He did not want to accidentally hurt anyone. There are many other examples of werewolf stories, too. Werewolf legends have been around for thousands of years, and people still enjoy them today.

GLOSSARY

cursed (KURST) When someone is cursed, he or she is harmed by an evil act or unfortunate event. In many stories, werewolves are cursed.

deformed (deh-FORMD) If a body part grows incorrectly, it is deformed. In many stories, werewolves look like deformed humans.

flesh (FLESH) Flesh is a term for skin and meat. In some legends, werewolves eat human flesh.

inspire (in-SPIRE) To inspire is to influence or bring about something else. Wolves inspire werewolf legends.

mythology (mith-AH-loh-jee) Mythology is a collection of stories that are not true but are believed or popular. The oldest werewolf legends come from Greek and Norse mythology.

predators (PRED-uh-turs) Predators are animals that hunt and eat other animals. Wolves are predators.

prey (PRAY) Prey are animals that get hunted or eaten by other animals. Sometimes wolves howl to show where prey is located.

TO LEARN MORE

In the Library

Castellano, Peter. *Werewolves*. New York, NY: Gareth Stevens Publishing, 2016.

Eschbach, Christina, and John Willis. *Werewolves*. New York, NY: AV2 by Weigl, 2020.

Furstinger, Nancy. *On the Hunt with Gray Wolves*. Mankato, MN: The Child's World, 2016.

On the Web

Visit our website for links about werewolves:

childsworld.com/links

Note to Parents, Teachers, and Librarians: We routinely verify our Web links to make sure they are safe and active sites. So encourage your readers to check them out!

INDEX

appearance, 6, 8, 14–15

Greek mythology, 11

hallucinations, 19
Harry Potter, 21
howling, 4–6, 17
hypertrichosis, 19

lycanthropy, 18–19

moon, 4, 8, 12, 17, 21

Norse mythology, 11

South America, 12, 14

transformation, 8, 11–12, 21

Wolf Man, The, 20
wolves, 4–6, 11–12, 14, 17, 18

ABOUT THE AUTHOR

Emma Huddleston lives in Minnesota with her husband. She enjoys running, swing dancing, and writing books for young readers. She thinks legends about creatures are fascinating!